The Goose Woman

Jane Kirwan

Published by Blue Door Press

Copyright © 2019 Jane Kirwan

Cover images by Aleš Macháček

Cover design by Pavla Ezeh

All rights reserved.

ISBN-13: 978-1-9164754-7-2

also by Jane Kirwan

Stealing the Eiffel Tower   1997

The Man Who Sold Mirrors   2003

Second Exile (with Aleš Macháček) 2010

Born in the NHS (with Wendy French) 2013

Don't Mention Her   2017

Stories & Lies (with Pam Johnson and Jennifer Grigg) 2018

For Roxy, Scarlett, Samuel, Lucas, Veronika, Tereza, Ozzy

ACKNOWLEDGMENTS

Thanks to the editors of Acumen, Magma, The Literary Bohemian, Literární revue *Weles,* The Hippocrates Book of the Heart, to Jane Duran and her group and ReWord. Particular thanks to Pavla Ezeh for her patience, Kate Tintner for her encouragement, and to Pamela Johnson and Mavis Gregson for their eagle eyed editing, and, of course, Aleš Macháček.

Nearly 20 years ago, after a casual *yes, why not,* Jane Kirwan and Aleš Macháček moved from sofas and central heating in North London to a ruin in Central Bohemia. No electricity or water or weasel-free room to sleep. The spirit of the space was then, and is still – long after her death – a goose woman. She weaves in and out of these poems, connecting the place to the poet's roots in the West of Ireland; she is there as they build, transform, make a home, she's still there as they take over her cottage, get older, become grandparents, and she is mostly quiet, only the occasional cackle.

1

This is the House

Exiled	13
Goose Woman	14
I Am Slabce	15
Bohemian Redstart	17
Wanting Milk in Many Voices	18
A Clothes-Line Near Rousínov	19
Gossip	20
Visitors	22
Tunnels	23
Hitch-Hiker	24
On Looking Up and Measuring Chimneys	26
Renovation	27
According to St Teresa this is the Middle of Europe	28
Recycling the Plastic Kremlin Barometer	30
Tail that Casts a Shadow	32
Conversation about Plumbing	33
This is the house that Aleš built	36
End of March in Slabce	37

2
Where They Blossom

Lost	39
To Do a Journey, or to Make a Stop	40
Gift	41
The Goose Woman Considers	42
Where They Blossom	43
Map of Where They Love	44
Blueberries	45
Not Being Sure About Love	46
Your Jacket	48
Anticipation	50
Doppelgängers in the Garage-Cafe	51
Consummation	52
According to the Police	53
Waiting for Fireworks in Český Krumlov	54
Forest	55
Recognising a walk	56
Afternoon Tea with Vladimír	58
On the Move	60

3

is this what you wanted

Borders	62
Taking the Sleeper from Kracόw to Prague	64
is this what you wanted	66
Trees on each side hold their breath	68
Sun on the Újezdec Road	69
The Man From Pavlíkov	70
Emptying the Barn	71
After Listening to the News	72
Confused by Time	73
Výměnek	74
The Traces She Left	76
Sheila	77
Gone	78

4

This Time It's Not Novák's Guitar

On Not Wanting Grandmothers	80
This Time It's Not Novák's Guitar	81
Her Language	82
Forcing Rhubarb	83
Doing a Granny-Knot in Numbers	84
Those Left Behind	85
Ned Bolingbroke's Three-Card Trick	86
The Last of the O'Connors	88
Arklow Sugar Bowl	89
On Not Wanting a Grandchild	90
User-name	91
Kate's long black hair falling forward	92
Central Bohemia	93
Paying attention	94
The Mackintosh	95
Leaving Slabce	96
Destination	98

Notes

1

This is the House

Exiled

Not the goose woman or cherry trees
or you
but the wild bees
who made a home in the abandoned mole-tunnels

their gusts of desperation
fussing at wet concrete
poured to fix a badminton pole
an agitated magnified humming

for days   their persistence
buzzing into each other the apple trees their frenzy
hissing at the ground for the missing
their mystification

Goose Woman

She half-closes the shed door, slots candles
into the holders, stuffs more into saucers of earth,
scoops away any straw.

She lights them all and then
kneels among her geese with their gobbled grumbles.
They are beautiful, but brainless

dazzled to an almost quiet.
This is not about getting acquainted
with any feather-winged archangel

but herself.
One of these afternoons when she creaks to her feet,
kicks the geese outside

they will fly up,
in a great fluttering cloud of white.

I Am Slabce

I am Slabce and I have 730 inhabitants
who all go to Croatia in August or stay in their gardens
and eat cucumbers. My one road needs resurfacing,
my river is a kilometre away and massages are available
in my town hall (actually the castle) every Monday.
I will call my country-music festival a secret
and put posters everywhere, even in Pavlíkov.
I am Slabce and do not trust anyone from Svinařov.
Each of my houses has crystal looted from the castle
and a linen napkin. All residents are called Novák
and only thirty of them go to the flower show
in the Kulturní dům, twenty nine of those
put their lupins in for the competition.
Point-one-percent are drug dealers and thirty-percent
are having an affair. The mayor is always occupied.
All my voters are Communist and voted for Babiš
except Mr Novák, and we are proud of it.
If you want any soil, or gravel, or sand,
contact my deputy mayor on a Tuesday and he or his son
will turn up on Friday week.
My river has many trilobites, my forests
many mushrooms, the mill by the Slabecký stream
has bullet holes and is falling down;
a Kalashnikov killed a woman, her child
and her lover so we do not go there, it's haunted
and the nettles are nose-high.
I did have a pub, I had two but now we sit at home
with Staropramen from Tesco. My street goes

from the carpenter's three wolves past the tree-man
as far as the 'used-car' collector on the road to Újezdec
avoiding the lake that my mayor says
'is not his responsibility'. I could go on
but am a quiet place with little conversation,
I might look surly but check my newsletter,
it's often delightful: deaths, marriages,
firemen get-togethers plus dates of the annual ball
held every second month.

Bohemian Redstart

All summer
we can't use that door to the kitchen

tuck tuck
he clicks gently
bobs
    on the
roof

cautious

checks his mate settled under the eaves by the woodshed
anchored   by a tail of debris
keeping the mess
            in balance
(against the draught along the veranda)

fledglings leave
then   another nest
     more eggs

occasionally
we catch him   in flight
     flash of red   dandy flash   that   *watch me*

Wanting Milk in Many Voices in Bohemia

Jarda asks for mléko. The toddler, Milo, yells milch,
mjölk, hurls his cup. All spilt. His mother mops it up,
hisses: *pas de point de pleurer*.
I press a switch, collect tea bags, mugs, sugar.

The kettle pitches in like a person wailing,
finds peace as it reaches the boil
– my mother's battered aluminium perched
on a gas ring, cap rammed to the spout lop-sided

metal shuddered, steam whistled, an ear-splitting shriek.
Hanna wants sója. The kettle stops gently,
not forbidding like Granny's black iron with its long spout,
low mutter, brooding all day on the range

then poured in a scalding arc over Darjeeling,
her tea darker than any made since, leaves scooped
from a chest, its jagged-metal rim, drift of dust and incense.

A Clothes Line Near Rousínov

The rope droops from the apple tree
– it should be taut with the cherry
but the cherry's trunk has split.

Clothes soak in a bowl by a wood pile
– the grass is hip-high,
pegs on the window ledge muddy.

There are no clouds but it won't happen
– song thrushes nest on the twin tub
and it's too green a spring to care.

A spring that will return again without us
with the same blossom as it was
for those who pegged overalls, vests

then left in a panic,
no time to drag clothes from a line,
their washing never collected.

Gossip

Because the goose woman stopped talking,
her son has brought her back for a visit.

She stoops by the shed – she'd sit there hours
in the dark – you show her an egg a weasel left.

She asks for her cat – most certainly dead –
that led eleven kittens out of our loft.

She frowns at the fence, points out the wire
her father fixed around the field when she was three,

the pear he planted a hundred years ago.
She's ninety-two, invites the boy with tattoos for coffee

– he drinks only tea and slivovic,
painted his pump near her door bright blue.

Her daughter-in-law heaves wheelbarrows
while her son advises you on the falling wall.

This summer, there are no hens, no geese.
In this heat, under the acacia, no longer the low murmur

when she gossiped with the postwoman:
the tone of their Czech was so familiar,

like Granny with Tessie outside The Hotel surveying
Main Street: *didn't she marry one of the Sligo Moores*

*and that one, a buck-tooth goat from Charlestown,
and herself no better than she ought to be;*

*he met her slaving in Brown Thomas, now she's so grand
she wouldn't piss the day of the week.*

Visitors

You promised Sami a mole;
he squats over a heap of soil, one of a row that stretch
like cowpats from the compost
to the dead beech – there are six, he's six.

He spreads his palms over the hole,
a midwife ready to slide in, lift this gift
from its world of life and birth,
its safety under roses, hazels,

out from its tunnels
while you block all exits,
concoct plots to stop these intruders.

It can tell the smell of you both,
will nuzzle for connections,
find its way underneath.

Tunnels

The moles are gone, or in hiding after Mita prodded
their tunnel: *Please be darlings and leave.*
The garden no longer looks bull-dozed. Mita might
have added: *You're not really wanted.*
So we needn't buy the solar-panel-driven deterrent?
Did she imply *This is not your home?* Is there somewhere
they can settle? Or is it because neighbours put poison,
the moles are missing, perhaps dead? Mita insisted
they'd understand and leave, these good-natured animals
prefer to be wanted, not happy that the mess – dying-
drying plants – is down to them. But where can they go?
They knew. This house was losing a garden,
Mita lost a house – her country went missing in '68,
an émigré for thirty years – now she'll buy a rucksack
and walk; she craves marshes, skeins of geese taking off,
a ripple through grasses, wave of lines through yellow.

Hitch-Hiker

Vladimír was laid off from the coal mines in Kladno
when you offered him a lift, then a job.

I live on the edge of he'd never say where.
You gave him money and clothes in exchange

for pummeling clay between the beams of a barn
or chopping wood, brick laying or general digging

since everything was collapsing into the lane
and needed shoring up with more than Honza's car jack.

All day Vladimír wandered around humming
leaving his good clothes, ancient jeans, stained anorak,

with his lemonade on the table in the yard,
always wore your filthy-baggy-greasy red sweat-pants,

ripped from hip to knee, torn possibly-once-white t-shirt
showing his belly and podgy arms and general defeat.

Though he was a big man he seemed a bit like the last
of the fireflies – fewer and fewer each year – shifting

around as if without hope, only occasionally flashing
any light, but muted and lackadaisical.

He'd turn up each year, work his exact hours then drink
slivovic outside Novák's, offering odd bits of gossip

about us, before going home each night to the forest
until the summer he didn't come back.

On Looking Up and Measuring Chimneys

Medieval builders set fire to scaffolding
to harden the plaster, so it is you light the stove
and we watch smoke curl from the new chimney

wait for the last bat to flee a Pentecostal spire,
decide the copper cap is too high.
I drive to welders in Lubná.

Along the way, village roofs have clay pots topped
by flat or curved metal, and the churches – peeling paint,
cracked stucco – have red or green onion domes.

Each week I can see from the yard a priest
– Carrefour bag, brown suit, trainers – unbolt the gate
of our own unloved Svatý Václav, ring out the bells.

Old women shuffle to Mass, staring down at a track
that is steep, neglected. They're compelling.
I hesitate – the urge to join those grandmothers –

and look up. Smoke idles from the chimney
to the limes, a perfect spiral giving a perfect halo,
copper floats at a perfect height.

Renovation

She has left a trail of cleared-out lofts, smart
with white walls, picture windows. No locks,
there are staircases down – ways out –
and not just fancy attics but basements with armchairs,
floral paper, wall TV and books.

Bit by bit old spaces resurface: here's a room
with a bolted hatch, cobwebs, bottles of maraschino
or this cellar with its metal safe, slope of coal,
smell of gas. Ceilings are lower, concrete walls sweat,
nobody is around, the handle has snapped off the door.

She'll restore this one with its rusting bucket of boots,
boxes of bullets, stained flag. She has tried.
They're entitled to lock her in,
through the keyhole she can see an open mouth,
a tongue, some tiny teeth.

According to St Teresa this is the middle of Europe

The nun waiting at the kitchen door is a saint.
Judgement Day she warns *but we haven't turned up
where we're buried, more like half-way.*

She's drunk two bottles of Frankovka,
claims to be Teresa from Avíla – who travelled a lot.
When trumpets sound, she's certified saved.

I put on the kettle – I'm not sure I'm dead –
pour us both gin, wonder who's the guy in tears
in the goose woman's shed teaching himself Czech?

Poor Bonaparte she says *is between Moscow and St Helena,
so nervous, he's learning the accusative case.*
When did he die? My sense of France is vomit on the ferry,

free-wheeling a Solex down a hill near Rheims,
almost to Vichy, even Dreyfus,
not back to him, let alone any chat about Spain in 1505.

Teresa pursues me with Slovak cheese
immerse yourself pet in difficulty.
I go for bread, collect another table, thank Providence

most Born Again are tiny,
all in the garden waiting for judgement.
Napoleon's doomed whisper conscripts from Austerlitz.

Am I dead?
Is feeding them my test?
Teresa has found mushrooms, mottled and poisonous.

My sense of Czechs might stretch before Sixty Eight
to the Occupation and Terezín
to Masaryk, Němcová

but are there any Přemyslids here?
Whatever, this lot are hungry – I'll make soup.

Recycling the Plastic Kremlin Barometer

You coveted the goose woman's large garden
so when she died we bought her cottage
and ninety years of saucepans, choppers, spoons, knives.

You shook hands on the deal with her forester grandson
– he'd checked both tiny rooms, left her life behind,
goose-feather duvet plumped in a heap on her bed.

He'd ignored the photos, bundles of letters,
his children didn't fiddle to untie the string.
We no longer spy as she boots her geese from yard

to shed – her occasional grumbled dobrý den.
Should a shopping-trolley go to the dump?
Never again will she drag it down the front steps

past both Nováks, up the slope to the church and co-op.
We're decades too late to witness her set off
for a day's work in the forest or hauling home a cart of hay.

The church clock tolls every quarter,
the moment exhausted before the next bell.
Muddy clogs were junked in the loft and Rudé právo.

I bin farm accounts, a hair-roller, some suntan oil Jardin.
We hold our breath, wait to count the time –
each stroke seconds too late, each hour has that delay.

You claim her tin beakers for blueberries, her milk churns,
ditch a comb, eat some pickles; you dither
a blotched mirror over Keep, break a spider's thread.

I throw away goose feathers,
save a plastic Kremlin barometer topped by a red star.

Tail that Casts a Shadow
Greek: skíouros, shadow-tailed   Middle English: squirel,

It threads the birches lightly, loops, dives;
its black eyes trimmed with white,
the rest is golden-red.

He sees it too, stands with her at the window,
pulls a knife through a loaf held to his chest

and there's a shadow. The man, the bread
are tucked together, utterly foreign –

the same slice to the body as locals cut salami
on childhood trains in France.

Impossible romances survived in that fleeting
landscape, those towns, red tiles on the roofs

– *Red Roofs*, the title of a story book,
on the cover a cottage buried in a valley

where a red squirrel made sandwiches
for the good child, not for the wicked –

what had she seen? The gesture of a knife,
his certainty – the shadow of a tail,
golden-red in a cradle of green, red not grey.

Conversation About Plumbing

*Next summer you'll have a pond, I'll channel it
from the well.* Next summer we'll lounge on the moon
– look at that shed, your pipes end in air.
But see those beaks: redstarts nesting in the jasmine.

And they need water. Pumps in Italian movies look easy,
years cursing ours – rusted and stuck,
it needs back-break priming before pitching with buckets
a hundred metres to the kitchen.

I'll fix gutters, then we'll recycle.
When at last it rains, it pounds the ground,
makes a ditch by the dump.
There's the start of a pool, I'll shift that old stove.

You load the firebricks first – they're heavy –
stripped from the fire-chamber and double oven
then you lean again
to take their weight in the wheelbarrow

and balance it along planks across the yard,
arms tense, knuckles white,
you shoulder it up and forward
to release the bricks where the lane dips.

Back you go, many times then loop a rope around
the cast-iron stove over the full-length cast-iron

heating plate, keeping shut the faulty ash-door
fixing wooden blocks to act as levers

to push it gutted up the slope to
Jandra's dump   half-way   you turn
to speak

        but can't   pale   sweating
            your hair sticking up.

The dump has gone and so have the puddles.
Moles tunneling below your bushes drain any water;
you think you can sort it with butts and barrels
and pumps. You connect Albutt by the blueberries

to Cherrybutt, then Romantic butt and Celibutt one
– when Celibutt two in the second cellar flooded
it fed the nasty neighbour's well.
But the drought? Too late for the occasional bucket.

So, like the exhausted petals on the roses
– the glory of last week's crimson irrelevant
as you snap off the dead – you say *No more*.
The aquefers are dry.

It used to be compromise,
the same way that after a late frost the walnut
gave new leaves but no fruit
or lizards persisted in the window

even if the pipe where you found the crack was patched
but the gooseberries are pathetic, the pond a myth,
you'll focus on winter:
on thermostats, stop-cocks, u-bends and boilers.

One warm room, one Limoges tea-cup
was never enough,
you'll make this house a circle,
take warmth from a recycled stove, a promise of home.

This is the house that Aleš built

and these are the tiles that wait for the roof
to go over the walls that Aleš bricked
to hold the doors that keep out the deer
that chewed the bark from his walnut trees
and these are the mice that nibble foundations
to cushion their beds with polystyrene
the swifts nicked to soften their nests
in this a house that needs more mesh
to shift the weasels who try to slide west
as far as the bedroom to eat the wiring
all in the house that Aleš built
with the leak he's fixed and fixed and fixed
while this is the maiden all forlorn
slutty in the hammock so weary and worn
here he comes all tattered and torn
to kiss this missy who's waited since dawn
she huffs off to make coffee
and growl at the cat who had mauled the rat
who has licked all the bottles
that hold up the house that Aleš built.

End of March in Slabce

There'll be no leaves,
the walnut trees will drip black ribbons –
blossom killed by frost last May. The lane will be mud,
squelching with slush and rotten pears,
we'll need our boots. I'll turn on the water,
count the mole-hills;
you'll take apples to the horses in the field,
some roses might have survived.
You'll go to the bottom lane, switch on the electricity,
my lavender and herbs will be dead.
We'll light the stove and air the bedding
then stop to watch the red squirrel
leap through the silver birch.
Roxy's plastic bucket will be by your blueberries.
You'll say the raspberry bushes have signs of life,
the lilacs are thriving
and start to prune the apple trees. I'll clean the fridge,
put coffee in the pot, find the sweater I lost at Christmas.
We'll stand under the old cherry, look out at the forest,
mist under the junipers,
the woodpecker will have started prodding the lime.
You'll say you're giving up on garlic.
It will be so quiet.

2

Where They Blossom

Lost

I spot someone in a headscarf, boots, smock,
harvesting the ditch,
show her my map
– its line to the horizon of a possible track.
She clutches my arm. Is she a witch?
Not there! I pull free, say *Thanks.*
Once over the rise the path is along the bank,
it follows the stream into birches
finally to the river.
The forest seems cautious. With her
foraging riches
far behind me, I stop near a fallen tree,
check for ants and sleep.

There is you, there is a bridge.

I wake, no bridge, my hands empty, river in flow
and I find a trail, return – not slowly –
through Újezdec
where the hen-woman warns *be lazy,
stay by the stove, the woods are full of crazies.*
And I go home quickly
because you had gestured to your chest
as I slept,
had appeared on the opposite ridge
then crossed over,
passed me your heart.

To Do a Journey, or to Make a Stop

The Bohemian says *I don't do houses*
as he potters about breathing garlic and forests.

Czech has the same word for *do and make*
as in *we don't do gods or goods*.

Well I don't do love, or sweet home she declares
(as in war and peace).

It's not their wandering but the stopping,
the elaborate set-up of defences,

greasy-spoon halts, barricades with deckchairs,
sea front benches, an occasional oasis

until at last he starts building
and they strip beneath willows, he whispers

let your doing fill me. Let all that made you
settle into us. Do me, lásko, make me.

Gift

A strong and steady man is spraying her roses,
has left her strawberries picked near her window
dipped in honey and soured cream

– it is not as the gale rocks the oak
this man rocks her
nor as in a cradle –

he moves from barn to house, radio in his pocket,
blocked off by headphones.
He's solid like the bath he fitted when she was away

the house he built, the balcony,
the square of his shoulders, like the foundations,
the spade he forces into soil

– it's rock as at the sea-side, peel off
the cellophane, his name printed
all the way through.

The Goose Woman Considers

She leaves her turquoise costume on a hook
above the stove, takes Rizlas, a book,
her shag tobacco, goes outside, settles
in the waist-high grass. Unfettered
by stays, she tucks her feet to her lap
like the Mahatmas, naked save her hat
– a black affair with net and lace –
rubs resin into tobacco on the paper,
flicks away fluff, dandelion clocks,
licks joins with the tip of her tongue, lops off
the ends, adds to her hoard. He comes
to her silently, his rose-aroma the same;
all her roll-ups are lost.

Where They Blossom

When I fail to find the bush of perfect flowers
seen the day before as I walked from Lubná,
I say this female flourishes more in cities.

I'm content to merge grey into buildings,
rumble with buses, breathe diesel fumes.
You prefer quiet, rural is peaceful,

the daily battle with moles, slugs,
the starlings who stole the cherries for your jam.
The lost bush was near the slope of aspen,

their trembling leaves flashing white like late blossom.
I say this female is happy
where there are cafés, theatres, intrigues, plots.

You say the country has lots of plots
and for my bush you'll need compost, seeds,
and a few old windows to make a greenhouse.

Map of Where They Love

He's asked for a map of where they love

she finds paper, crayons indigo the Rajasthan rug.
He climbs to the loft, opens the sky-light, calls:
distance gives scale

and she marks out grids,
lengthens a few for strangeness. Too quick.
She needs the moment she cleans the kitchen table

and he mops the floor – closing cupboard doors
on bowls, plates – when a space opens out.
He wants her to mark where the heart is.

Start again and clearer, make it nearer home.
She traces at the edge the path she laid
when she blocked his drains

with reckless use of cement and stones,
colours it blue; inks in green the track
they take barefoot through nettles

past a wood to the lake rimmed with bull-rushes;
she etches a dive so deep,
no borders can be seen.

Blueberries

You feed them all summer with coffee dregs
kept for you by the woman in the garage,

doctor the soil with sulphur, regulate
the water, net the bushes against starlings.

Every dawn your pilgrimage to check them out.
Roxy and Sami race through the fruit trees,

hopeful and forgiving; they shout *nearly ready*
expect any second grey will turn blue.

A few are left for me on the kitchen table,
these pallid spheres should be indigo and sweet.

How to suggest natural might be inadequate?
Each smooth solid berry has a necklace and cap

– water-speckled, dusty – not precisely a treat
but oh to be watched like that.

Not Being Sure About Love

I pull off my boots, announce I've found *true love*
and you're impressed, after all

we were both born in the year of the dog.
I describe my hero appearing out of the blue

at the top of the lane from Pavlíkov, ears cocked.
It hadn't even barked, was rummaging in the grass

then stopped, ran straight to the path and me.
You say a child walking it got bored

or its pensioner-owner was felled by a deadly mushroom
or more probable still, it was a menace and abandoned.

Whatever, the beauty stayed at my side, technicolour-clean,
head-over-heels and trusting.

It didn't even whimper at the Alsatian
millimetres from snaffling its muzzle

or the demented hounds pounding behind the fence.
They'd have snacked it alive,

not recognised it as pure transcendence.
I did suspect you might object

especially when in Zavidov it meandered all over the road
causing a screaming-choir of tyres, brakes and curses;

my sweetie needed a lead.
I started home cross-country.

So, where is it now?
I lost it.

Or, to be honest, in Hvozd I hid behind a wall
and watched it trot off after three girls with rucksacks.

Your Jacket

There must be a way that I can leave this,
see the sky again, but the exit
has drifted up through mist

– rumoured to the sixteenth floor
or beyond one of those disgruntled doors.
The fog's getting worse, corridors

don't connect,
lockers are blocked, stairs wrecked
– no point relying on lifts, better to expect

the ones that say up, to go down – all signs
are indifferent or hostile
and the children who gave directions lied.

All these nights,
no hope catching the train underlined
in the script, while tight

inside the garden trapped under the roof
are stacked a thousand parachutes.
Go back, retrace footsteps, prove

there once was an entrance
– days can be sharper, more intense –
prove I'll have confidence

to speed out of the city,
seeking you, the gift
of you – a sun in flames through a drift

of autumn trees – or go home, to back there,
your jacket on a chair,
knowing you are upstairs.

Anticipation

The pale-blue fabric with patterns like crystals
on an icy window
rippling from a washing line tied
between the silver birch and lime

is the same as the material kept in a drawer
that as a child, alone and feverish
restless in my parents' bed,
I needed a stool to reach.

This remnant of the neighbour's curtains
in this sun, at this height, brings – no blink between –
that high-temperature-urgency, metal angles to my mind
and yearning.

Was it organdie or lace or georgette?
It was lost, never made a dress, never worn
as a ballerina or at a party. Waiting
and so it remained as potential.

Now this, pegged on the line near the birch
– its worryingly small leaves – a delicate sky-blue,
it flutters, all rustle, the same craving,
thunder over the woods and heat, rain coming.

Doppelgängers in the Garage-Cafe

Someone has asked her if her double is cool.
The boy with soft dark hair, soft pale hands, answers
mine's a volcano of feeling. All turbulence.
He's hunched over a fourth brandy: *it's my subconscious
talking to the conscious and no,
I wouldn't sleep with an automaton.*
Zdeněk, eating ketchup with French fries, mutters
I've no distinct other but have a fluctuating concept of self.
The barman appears, she knows him and he knows this
– he works in Prague with Charles.
She says *It's uncanny, there must be two of you.* He smiles,
asks what she wants. Didn't Charles owe him money?
What if their doubles are weighed, will any shift the needle?
Do they exist? Why does she think of Macbeth?
The barman wouldn't accept her double as convincing
– it's a witch, all rat's tails and resentful.
Consciousness is a fact he says. Or did he mean conscience?
The boy has drawn a picture of a girl: *Me*, he says
then takes a knife, stabs the heart. *And authentic.*
The barman whispers: *It could be said Charles cut off his nose
to spite, who is it do you think?* Or did he just say
Do you want another single of Beefeater gin?

Consummation

After he left, the house is silenced, emptied,
a few feathers, some bones

until the middle of one night it starts,
through walls, pipes, the place becomes pigeon

an earthy, merging, vibrating throb
starting long before dawn

and she races up nine flights,
catapults stones into the dark – the sky sullen, bruised –

she shoots air-pellets, feather-tipped darts,
wills arrows to wing their way home

but it does not stop,
so she makes a scarecrow with his face

his sharp-dog features, scoops out the heart
then sits and waits

for him to come waltzing back
with his sack full of eggs.

According to the Police

Confirmed by the Ministry of the Interior,
Feodorovich Pututkin lives in this flat, has your identity,
is on his way.
Does he also have a square solid head
that pushed from your slight and slender mother,
did he tease her? And eat all the blueberries.
Your European ennui must pack its bag and leave,
in its place the steppes, growl of priests, belligerent bears.
The flat will smell of revenge and klobásky,
there'll be vodka for breakfast
and random violence.
But didn't you like vodka for breakfast?
He'll come and snore on the sofa, still holding his beer,
having left his boots in the fridge.
But don't you hang your boots over the stove?
If Feodorovich is you, who am I? Ivana Pututkin?
If so, I've skidded into the ditch
to leave that brat-bulk of a woman
with mop, bucket, and corsets who eats buchty all day.
Once she had blonde extensions, pearly-pink nails,
now her grandchildren sulk at summer camp
and chase old men up trees;
Feodorovich has been paying your bills,
he is waiting downstairs.

Waiting for Fireworks in Český Krumlov

Beside her, below the castle, three jesters slurp ice-cream,
a unicorn gossips to monks with beer-barrel bellies,
a Renaissance physician with a dildo pisses into the river.

Masked men wear leather shorts and bibs
– socks are cut to show the menace of their calves –
above them are a thousand windows honeycomb-pocked.

This is close to the border – she doesn't fit, it's fake,
a lonely bear-pit at the gate, no buckets of hot pitch.
These drunken souls will groan and wobble home.

A light in a window, he's up there, her alchemist,
her technician with his plots that liquefy the guts,
his timing – finger on whatever button – his plan.

He tamps down gunpowder, sets fuses, welds frames,
starts fires for martyrs. The clock strikes, the sky explodes,
a hundred rockets whine in parachutes of citrus.

Stars are hearts, diamonds slide, rake skin,
slither under muscle, vibrate. All pulse in chorus, break
their dark to light; at midnight he trembles her awake.

Forest

after Anselm Keifer Royal Academy 2014

Until that room in the gallery – a wall of glass
encasing webs of hazel branches,
everything still,
snow smothering the ground –

not until then,
seeing the remnants of some hut,
a feeding station for deer,
scattered boxes, bee-hives

was it possible for fake
to become forest,
more need than real, and to feel ice-chill,
for the floor to shiver

and to be clear how the trees
 – aloof, a regularity of trunks soaring up,
  stretching back an immeasurable distance,
  blocking the sky –

in their indifference
made it reasonable to take the wrong path,
our tracks concealed in minutes.

Recognising a Walk

A man appears ahead – Újezdec is snowed-over,
frost grips the trees down to the ice-burdened river –

his black jacket, black cap sudden against a slate-sky,
he's alone in the forest shadow, almost glides

assumes this his own solitary track.
She recognises his back,

she recognises his walk.
Aged four, she'd left her grandmother's house, its talk

and she had walked. She takes possession of his stride
– it's in her muscles, a strength she recognises

that keeps her trailing him through birch, hornbeam,
past the silenced stream.

She follows his boot prints until he disappears in mist;
he's veered to the right. No reason to do this,

it's getting late. She stays straight.
The exhilaration as a child of being free to walk away.

Snap. An explosive crack
then splintering bark.

It can't be him, more likely deer.
The trail no longer falls, it rises, turns, becomes unclear

then stops,
a steep drop to the frozen Berounka.

Not a sound in the enclosing dark.
Blundering through brambles, she hunts for a path

curses her stupidity, heart racing,
bushes thin then widen to a clearing; beyond acacia

is a three-sided shack, beneath lime trees
the man tilts a cup over boxes, he is feeding his bees.

Afternoon Tea with Vladimír

When Vladimír reappears after ten years,
says come for tea, we come.

We set off past the collective farm,
trudge several kilometres through forest

to a clearing among birches.
Behind a bonfire, indistinct in sun-light

are two benches and a plate of klobásky,
packs of cigarettes, tin-ashtrays and vodka.

Inside a hut are heaps of smoke-soaked bedding
– no pot of tea, no cucumber sandwiches.

Vladimír introduces his fellow trampers
– two men who look like trees.

One offers to take the children for a trek
and we say yes. They're away for hours

– we scream their names into the distance –
until just before dark he returns,

one child on his shoulders, the other two
dragging compulsory wood for the fire.

These men use a country-wide network –
odd jobs and forest huts, keys hidden.

Their arms are branches, bodies knotted,
leathered skin – an ease of beer and slivovic.

Vladimír has found casual work for a zoo
near Plasy, building cages.

On the Move

When I dump my bag, the furniture faces away;
it was once promiscuous with its promise of comfort.

A nail-varnish stain on the sofa is new, a table chipped –
life has continued here, but not mine.

In another country, a clock from a divorce ticks on;
why hang on to stuff, it only sulks?

My mother's chairs, her table, are back there,
a monk's chest. Is that chest too battered, too big

and too late to find its place?
As a child I'd climb inside, pull down the lid,

breathe into the dark and sleep.
All I can do for any of this is dust.

3

Is This What You Wanted?

Borders

We stopped for the night in Athens, going home
or heading north for what was home at the moment.
We drove into Macedonia – regular yellow fields.
Customs were quicker than last time.
Four hours in a traffic queue among the wooded slopes
before Montenegro; a low wall separating us
from the drop to the valley. I thought I could live there.
You said at least it was smoother than that mountain road
into Turkey: pot holes, fake border, men with Kalashnikovs.
We paid all the tolls with credit cards,
we were hungry. The hotel was on the motorway near Skopije.
It had balustrades and porticoes, an empty car-park,
a dining room more like a ballroom, an acre
of empty tables, two dead sparrows near the cash desk.
A waiter appeared. He straightened a hundred chairs,
unhappy in his white nylon jacket, then said
nothing was available. Maybe Schnitzel.
In the distance near the sign to the Jacuzzi,
four middle-aged men drank beer with chasers.
Before crossing into Hungary we searched
for a place to sleep, Serbian villages were shuttered, silent.
The young men waiting for a room ahead of us had guns
in their jacket pockets. It was nearly midnight,
no cars, no one on the streets.
We talked of a detour to see the wild horses, skipped Budapest.
In our rented Fabia, we decided to drive through the night,
I marvelled at the neatness of the countryside.
As we crossed the border at Znojmo, fields

gave way to casinos strung for miles,
night-clubs flashed orange, purple, puce.
We stopped for petrol and coffee. It was 4 am.
Two girls waited near the tyre-pressure gauge,
another in stilettos lounged by the pumps.
The road was empty, the car and lorry-parks full,
number plates mainly Czech and Austrian.
At regular intervals, on both sides,
ten-metre-high inflated women with legs spread wide
swayed slightly in the warm night air.
The smell of diesel and burgers. All neon-enhanced
and available. We were heading for Jihlava
– it sounded like Jehova – but never found it.
A juggernaut overtook us, avoiding motorway taxes
it stormed through the dead villages.

Taking the Sleeper from Kracόw to Prague

While passengers for Budapest tucked themselves into bunks,
we'd waited on a dark platform. Our carriage was locked

> her father is disappearing, has sent gentle and calm
> instructions; he's in Cork, wants everything
> in order– his words come from a Cork childhood,
> Venetian blinds, sunlight and sin –
> all for his pleasure, plate piled with drisheen
> like the soft inedible pork sausage of Poland.
> Her father is tall, punctual, is always locking and

the short and smiling inspector was late;
he arrived in a fluster, crumpled white shirt, bulging belly,
his buttons undone as if the real version was drunk somewhere,
this one turfed out of a props cupboard.
You haven't spoken to me before?
His cap was the size of a serving plate;
he unlocked all doors, posted destinations,
he squinted at tickets, waved his arms.
As you like, let me help. He clambered up ladders,
checked bottom bunks *Good Morning, good morning.*
It was not yet midnight. *Anything you want.*
He had lost his spectacles; his cabin was a mess:
dirty plates, half-eaten sausage, unmade bunk, spilt beer.
The other man mixed up these tickets he said
in five languages to whoever didn't understand.

Of course, she thought as she slept,
that other man strolling away – his strange cap –
her father dawdling down the train corridor.

is this what you wanted for Milada
Labyrinth, Tate Modern, 2018   Ilya and Emilia Kabakov

at the distant end in the gloom is a corner
beyond it another

corridor   another corner   another
long airless corridors   get

more narrow   locked doors no exit
a labyrinth

this is   in this dark   the same
as searching those hospital corridors

Milada was dying in some ward
down one of many cul-de-sacs

the walls are lined with photos of almost-ruins   and words
a woman's life translated above picture frames

The artist Ilya –
his mother's life   hunted homeless, starvation –

Milada's story   the same blocked Bolshevic corridor
            this is art

and not someone else's   we are reading this wall
all exhibits

in the distance a man sings – mournful remote –
Milada would have wanted to witness him singing

corridor after corridor
makes a shape of suffocation

'is this what you wanted?   please visit me'
the mother's final words above the last picture frame

looking for Milada
her fight to push her story through her life

the music is louder   the last sentence
above the last sepia photograph 'is this what you wanted'

a barrier at the end
Milada said 'please visit me'

behind the barricade someone's singing a requiem
she wanted to tell me her life

Trees on each side hold their breath

Is this her *dharma* on the road
to Rakovník or her *kharma*

as a car from the other direction skids
an inch from the bonnet,
swerves in reverse?

It misses her back by a blink,
crashes into the ditch
– trees on each side hold their breath.

Her daughter's email from Koh Lanta
be in the moment, Madre... stretch time

as it must stretch now
– she doesn't want the child to drive, not ever –
his speed, her speed, each fraction

of a second exact to pass
between both inevitable impacts

or more that it is *dharmakaya,*
the mind slipping on ice.

Sun on the Újezdec Road

There's a centipede
resting in the middle of the tarmac
red and black and gorgeous
enjoying the heat through each hair of one hundred delighted feet
ignoring the woman
who stares at the cool ditch
dithering about shifting it to safety
away from its moment.

The Man from Pavlíkov

You are pruning the cherry trees, checking for blight,
stop to ask *Can you Google living wills?*

I find Advance Directive
which sounds a bit like the man from Pavlíkov
has turned up, slightly drunk, with a chainsaw
and is cutting down the lime tree.

*Just print out a form. Try Help the Aged and keep it simple,
I'll need you as my ally.*

So, you won't even fight
or do a Canute fending off the ocean with an open palm,
make me print some half-cocked, half-arsed bundle sealed
with brittle wax and ribbon, words that never blossom,
ribs so tight the light's scarpered, leave me clutching in my fist
a ghost of a goal with a mess in the orchard

and I'll be the muggins who has to do whatever.
Well you say *it's sensible.*

Emptying the Barn

I spot you dragging scales that once weighed hay
to the bonfire.
Not that!
Make hay while, but it's sunset nearly.

You say *Why keep it?*
then dump it near the blighted nectarine.
The load-table just above the ground
is double – two one-metre-squares of pine

slide gently against each other
an upright rectangle – levers chains pulley
a maker's stamp: 803.
Because it's beautiful.

But is it? What skewed romance is this?
How does it work?
The fifth labour of Hercules had more dung
than dried-out grass, yet so valuable

it weighed as a life in the balance.
From the gate this reject looks like a gravestone.
Burn it.

After Listening to the News

Disturbed, like the crow I startled,
it dumped the tiny blackbird still alive
then settled, strutted, raked at wet leaves

or, on the lane from the Polish pond,
when a buzzard soaring away spotted me, it
looped back, dropped the guts of a newborn hare

a disturbance can be a slight ruffle
in the order of things, or can be the order of things

like those meals where president and guests
tear apart baby songbirds.

Confused by Time

Was it last August? This year or the year before,
the night of the Perseid shower?

We lay on a clear patch of grass
between the apple trees and hazels, watching the sky.

It's now October,
today's image of a collision between two neutron stars
has taken 130 million years to reach us.

Last summer's streaks of light, shooting across
that endless above, were already dead.

It seemed inconceivable – you rolling over to hold me –
that this should stop
or that – me spooned into the arc of your body

both of us earthed –
and feels now not like last summer

but 130 million years ago, folds in time
as we picked up the blanket, went inside.

Výměnek

The days are getting shorter. She does try to normalise, act
cautious. She'd been looking at a documentary – is watching

a life more realistic than having to live one? But it's snowing,
not even seeing flakes drift lightly slows anything.

They are moving into a výměnek, decorators are coming,
she must protect the books. Better to be a lover of books,

she doesn't need to read them all. Someone somewhere
wrote *children are a burden people keep repeating*.

There is snow at the top of the stairs where the corner turns
and it's dark. She'd always wanted it utterly dark, tucked in,

protected, if you touch something soft then scream.
When the arm of a burglar came in the window over her bed

she couldn't make a noise. *What colour was it?* said
the policeman. What colour's her claw reaching for a wall?

The brain changes. It's clear that this new place is another
extension of the same old labyrinth

much like attempting The Pilgrim's Progress as a teenager,
thinking it should be a good read. And it wasn't.

A sinking inevitability. Or Comenius? What about Love?
They then came to a gate called Discipline,

*they had magnificent libraries and they pointed to the beauty
of their stacks.* A whole life and not reading any of it.

She can't slow any of this down, her lungs are full of feathers;
reading, as in having a map where bats dart at the words.

Those who know (ie planned this maze) provided logs for
the stove; snowflakes drift to a stop, the blackbird is singing.

Life as a crash, she knows to apologise but not how to brake.
Eke it out over the next few years, don't be a bother,

good will is not the same as love at all, it can turn on a coin.
Why think of this too late like the clown arriving

after the cake's been cut? Let's start again.
You come all this way to lie in the hammock, and it snows.

Traces She Left

We turn on the radio, go outside, find footprints,
from the thickness of air we'd known it was snowing.
The roof and sheds are smothered,
we wish we hadn't said we'd help.

It must have been her who leant on the window ledge
– those cigarette butts – nothing we could do.
The branches of rowan, tired with winter,
creak against the limes.

She's left a trail of burnt-out votive candles.
The path ends in a caked-over river – all this asks
to disappear, the usual ways have been too slippery.
She'd have said don't be nervous

be dazzled. We stand and do nothing,
the light expanding as just before a faint.
Footprints to a table there from last summer
– a white mound with bumps

where cups and plates are covered –
her track to the gate.
She left with the brandy and all the cutlery,
the iced earth blinds, the sky is yolk-yellow.

Sheila

In the top garden – a few moments past dusk –
my sister smokes a cigarette,
fireflies flicker in and out of the lilac.

It's warm, a shifty moon. She is here
in our garden
as fireflies drift down the path, circle her,

temporary and unearthly.
She has left
and so fast.

The glow of her cigarette, her right hand extended,
head tilted, measuring smoke rings
into the dark.

There is a pounding further up the lane,
it rumbles the ground
to a shudder,

        the drumming of hooves,
escaped heifers – massive, solid – thundering
down the slope to trample through our gate.

Gone

I swing dirty water across the yard
at the end of an autumn day –
the water mirrors the sky's crimson,
pools on patches between grass,
catches the ferns and dying roses,
wets the stones that step to the barn
and the boots that haven't been worn
since a wasp nest was found in the toe;
it sprays molehills and the sticky webs
that cling verandah rafters to beams,
splashes cracked tiles by the side door
with its ancient bolts, fissured wood;
the drops suspended in a red arc.

4

This Time it's not Novák's Guitar

On Not Wanting Grandmothers

After the goose woman's death I imagined her
coming back to find transcendence
with the geese in her third shed.

I saved her letters, books,
found balls of knitting wool, stored them in glass jars.
We moved into her cottage, still called it hers.

If honest, I should have catalogued my disgust
at her wizenedness, her immense age,
her surly effort to get to the Co-op

that dread of recognition
when I caught her kicking a duck
away from safety under the walnut.

The old crow hated anyone further than Rousínov,
especially Praguers who drove by her front step
when she was plucking a goose. She was all enemy.

I thought my horror of age started with her
then remembered being afraid of my grandmother
– so tall, so ancient – her sadness, her rage.

This Time it's not Novák's Guitar

You run out of the cottage, drop to your knees, hold up
your arms – Uilleann pipers bring the sea to Slabce –

and you beg them not to stop:
they must crack the heart of this dried-out street.

The music licks at doorways, leaks over cobbles, it aches
while three solitary pensioners scuttle indoors.

In the Co-op, the carpenter's daughter – pen behind her ear,
slicing sausage, generation after generation –

locks the shop windows, turns up Radio Blah,
clicks shut the blinds, yells *You idiot!*

Duped by that racket,
no better than a carp gulping air on the path!

Her Language

A black Bakelite phone rings in that kitchen
– my mother calling, she doesn't know me.
I face dirty laundry stacked into the alcove;
she makes no sense but it's her voice.

I wake, lose her – that tourist in Nádražní,
his accent, Mayo. How to retrieve it?
To have taped her telling a patient *don't fret*
then burying the phone in washing

and she off to chop onions, bash spuds
with us nearby, competing, arguing
– a few Northampton accents, others Irish.
Somebody laughs as we claim our songs

and she is singing along:
not the holiday splelch of rotten potatoes pelted
at the Kellys but voices
and of hers from an English scullery, no trace.

Forcing Rhubarb for Bernadine

You stop, look ahead *The next slope's easier.*
I describe my mother climbing this in bare feet
– she did it three times to pass exams.

Did she succeed? I don't answer.
My mother believed Croagh Patrick delivered miracles,
I don't, and I've no breath.

It's getting cold, on each side a rock-stricken drop,
through cloud a distinctly dull summit
– no doubt a McDonald's or posse of priests.

Flat on the scree, we scrabble up the vertical slope,
ask a descending bachelor *Does it get better?*
He's sliding down fast *It fecking does not.*

At last we make it,
totter through sunshine past nimble petitioners
to queue for the grey-stone toilet

and I remind you of the time in Slabce
you wedged roof tiles around rhubarb
like the goose woman's shawl

saying *light must come only from above*
and the rhubarb grew taller than us.

We share our water, admire the grey-stone chapel,
the clear view of Clew Bay.

Doing a Granny-Knot in Numbers

Granny lived in Number One Main St;
the front door to her huge dark rooms above the shop
was off Bridge St and the entrance to her Hardware & Bar
exactly on the corner.
Main St was where Aunt Jenny lived, six shops down
in Number Two, selling corsets and whiskey
by the alley where Ned Bolingbroke
bunked with Annie Horan.
Opposite, across this wide road that led down
and out of town, was Aunt Nancy's hotel, closed
by the authorities for after-hours gambling,
next door to Great-Aunts Kathleen and Peggy's grocery
– which did very well.
Uncle Joe had a draper's in Bridge St., half-way to the church
with a number I can't remember
and they are all gone, except for the ones we don't talk to.

Those Left Behind
Stone sculpture in Connemara   Richard Long

A line of stones discomforts
the irregular slate shelves
and splinters of rock

diminishes the natural
– the ground is cold here and damp,
the earth soft enough to die on.

No random scatter of pebbles on a famine field
with a fumble of rain on the hill
– wild disorder of the blue.

To compare is to make uneasy
– all we can do is witness,
our outlines are vivid, even the trees.

Ned Bolingbroke's Three-Card Trick

My mother said don't moan, you've no clue
what scapegoat means, and while over there
don't go near that villain Ned. And no gambling.
Her home, and no intention of going back.

A bus from Knock airport drops me by the hotel;
there's chat about a car, a Lexus with Dublin plates
thieved last week. She'd have said it was Ned's doing,
that he was cast out by the Big House

on the wrong side of the blanket. A bastard
and that's what the town still thinks.
But this was years ago, now she's not so sure
– all dead, her witnesses, those betrayed uncles.

Ned lives in the lane that links Bridge Street to Main.
The town split when they were children,
those for free trade and England in Main Street,
others Bolshie – like my father ferrying guns in Cork.

Surely by now Ned is dead?
He cracks open the door, he thinks I'm my mother:
Where the feck have you been?
He's leathered with age – thick breath, undrinkable tea –

starts on about looting of the Corner House
after Granny's death as if it was last week,
all that delft and gorgeous crystal,
that was a gifted woman, martyred herself for those girls

and then – this was last week – aiding cousin Nancy
liberate St Francis under the eyes of a priest
who'd demoted him, stuck the saint in a side chapel
– Mother of Jesus, the ignominy – and the statue given

as memorial to Nancy's dead brother.
Forty years Francis stood at the front by the altar
only to end rattled in the back of an old cart
to the Hotel and one of its landings,

the clergy choleric but fit to do nothing.
I have questions, Ned knows nothing of scapegoats
or otherwise, only I'm to carry a table to Kelly's,
help him play out his three-card trick.

The Last of the O'Connors

I'm alone at a table in Horkan's with a gin,
see only the backs of men hunched at the bar,
no fug of turf, that air of nostalgia has left
replaced the taxi-driver said by diesel
as he tuned the radio to funeral announcements.

Horkan's, where Great-aunts Kathleen and Peggy
wore hats and white gloves to read the *Western People*.
They sold butter here, across the road from Moore's
where Granny's name is no longer over the door,
counter on the wrong side, no shawled women

no snug, no grandmother. *So much smaller, dingier*
I said to the American smoking in the doorway.
At least Horkan's still has a grocery at the front
but they're out of black pudding.
Glints of light on bottles, on crystal

and remembering the stones mourners put on graves,
I buy a campanula to set on the step
of the abandoned and boarded-up hotel,
the last relative to live here has died, a boy, Conor,
a heart attack; this time the door's unlocked

his brother, Michael, is far inside, in the depths.
He takes the plant to the hall, puts it on Conor's piano
and as we talk an old man in tweed
comes from a door at the back, walks between us
and out of the front without saying a word.

Arklow Sugar Bowl

The china is crazed, the gold scratched,
sugar grains hardened, encrusted,

even the teaspoon is coated with white.
I thought I'd waltz in, hear *she's home at last!*

they ignore me,
no one is warming the pot, no one needs sugar.

I say who I am but
no one allows my romance about speeding away

they suggest I was pushed
– they're tapping Guinness, slicing ham, packing tea –

surviving the life they want to escape from,
don't give more than a casual fig about me.

On Not Wanting a Grandchild

I would have to raise her up
to the mahogany counter in the Corner Shop
– her solid surprising weight –
where she could spot through the hatch
the old gossips in the snug
with their whiskey-laced Camp coffee

and in the corner of the bar
luminous pates of three farmers
praying into their porter,
sunshine through stained glass blessing
crystal decanters, rows of spirits, ginger wine.

I would have to practice affection
with this godless-fickle-small stranger
looking at me warily – she's marooned,
perched too high, a Simeon in the desert –
accept her trust, not abandon her, smile
and walk off. I'd have to climb on a stool,

bring down the square biscuit tin, witness her
witness me open it, take out a fig-roll
and hand it to her, then scoop her up.

User-name

We're talking on Skype, Kate stands up
to show me her bump: What can she call you?

She means my user-name. I've had many,
the one now is pale drawn-out two-dimensional;
it speaks of grey corners.

Grey, as in this city, where sales assistants
look away and if I protest, they are dumbfounded.
Who is this mizzy shadow?

Oh, to be more substantial, like our neighbour Ivička
waiting at the top of the ladder
with a bucket of apples.

Don't throw any, Ivička, please,
the storks on the roof would shudder with the clatter.
I plan to fly away today, Ivička.

There'll be no embracing any user-name,
no letting the babe call me babička – I will resist.

Kate's long black hair falling forward

                                  my fear
while those dark-haired women are watching

as she, on her silver barge   pulls away
      they wait on that necklace of lakes

turquoise to emerald to indigo
each woman   each generation   held back

on a raft
        on their separate lake
by a dam of lilies   a fall of water

they wait
overlooked   by the black storks of Plitvice

as Kate gets further
                             and further

holding that hard kicking egg
and   I reach forward

touch her belly
and her daughter   kicks me back

Central Bohemia

this is the day the windows iced up
with you outside
      under frozen branches of the lime
you've stolen my blue woolly hat

I've turned off the news
squirrels line up nuts in the compost
blue tits shudder
as they queue for seeds from a rusted oven tray
      I must find another feeder

the trees are barren, the neighbours
– Bendls, Nováks – seem too near
      they want the borders closed
and you outside   scraping away at the glass
the day the windows iced up

Paying attention

Gooseberries, blackcurrants, cherries,
came as an abundant centre
to the long garden of Scarlett's first year
and then the summer stepped down
after apples and pears, the gold
that was a gift to this November child
who stretches time so beyond recognition
it makes no sense – plum plenty aeons ago.
She selects a blueberry left from August,
picks it up, examines, she is cautious, curious,
smashes it into her mouth
takes another   and another,
purple-faced babe, her endless blueberry world.

The Mackintosh

You are throwing away your old mackintosh,
I think. You might change your mind,
you are sorting,
three bags of bed-linen will go to Prague
– left over from clearing my mother's house.
The raincoat was once smart.
I like the way it hangs from shoulders
that are broad and trustworthy,
you dissembler you.
You seem so content as you pick and pack
as if released.
You keep the stripey sheets I rejected.
The mackintosh is musty green,
I bought it for you in a charity shop in Národní,
20 years ago; it was as good as new.
I like it because you look stylish, respectable,
a bit British.
A spy on the corner, a lit cigarette.
I make you walk ahead, I like looking at you
from the back.

Leaving Slabce

I've let the stove go out
– you want to stay all winter –

after coffee
we'll leave this freezing house

a bird slams against the glass door
lies stunned on the red tiles we laid last spring

not a shiver
in its blue-grey sudden-still body

so fast
that solid thump of muscle aimed at us

– last June a nuthatch knocked itself unconscious
against the loft window

dropped to wild grass
then plunging its claws into your broad earth-stained fingers

wedded itself, buried in
then sleepily

recovered to life   refused to leave
assessing (relaxed, appreciative) its post-shock landscape –

you say this feathered death is a starling
I disagree, double-check locks

while you go to bury the mess   do not say where
looking back at me with a query

as if I'd sent the bird
like a stone from your catapult

that should have flown smooth
but gave a shudder, a pause.

Destination

The bus driver will be irritable
and even though I'm the only passenger
he won't let me sit at the front
will not put on the heating
and even though he's not going on anywhere
he wants me off at the last stop
though I've nowhere to go
and he will park somewhere
behind the church or near the Co-op
and I'll have given up
it will be night, the one street completely empty
all the houses dark
no hint of that high-June-blue sky
but there will be fireflies between the lime trees
and I'll remember I love you.

Notes:

19. A Clothes-Line Near Rousínov
400 metres from the road between Slabce and Rousínov is a small abandoned Jewish cemetery. It has been tidied up over the last 20 years and some of the broken, engraved gravestones have vanished.

29. According to St Teresa this is the Middle of Europe
1968: Warsaw Pact Invasion.
1938: German Occupation. Terezín: a fortress town in Northern Czech was used by the Germans as a concentration camp and transit point for other extermination camps like Auschwitz.
Tomáš Garrigue Masaryk, born in 1850, the first Czechoslovak president, 1920-35.
In the battle of Austerlitz (Slavkov), 1805, the Austrian army defeated by Napoleon included many forced Czech conscripts. A description of the effect of conscription is in Božena Němcová's most loved book, *Babička,* published in 1855.
Přemyslids: This Bohemian dynasty started in the 9th century and ended with the death of Wenceslas 3rd, in 1306.

31. Recycling the Plastic Kremlin Barometer
Rudé právo: literally Red Law. Official government/party newspaper.

53. According to the Police
After a car accident the police took our IDs. Apparently Aleš' ID number and address were in the name of someone called Feodorovich Pututkin. It took much paperwork and eventual intervention by the Ministry of the Interior before Feodorovich was deleted.

66. is this what you wanted

After the '68 Soviet invasion, Milada Bejblíková, a senior hospital doctor in Prague, was sacked from her job and her husband Alois (Loyzic) – essayist and translator – was banned from academic work. It wasn't until the '89 Velvet Revolution that Loyzic's achievements were recognised; Milada never got her position back. In June 1990, as they were beginning to enjoy freedom, their car was smashed into by an army truck; Milada was in another ward, her legs in plaster and prevented by the staff from going to Loyzic, who died, aged 64, as she put it 'from medical neglect'.

Milada spoke only Czech. She vowed to devote herself, as Loyzic had done, to English; she visited Britain several times, met Loyzic's academic contacts, listened only to the BBC. Then she became ill, couldn't travel.

By 2002, she was in her seventies, housebound; I was living between Slabce and Prague when a friend introduced us. Milada only wanted to speak, hear, read, English. I visited her each week and we talked.

She was the most angry person I'd ever met.

In 2018, six years after Milada died, I was in London at an exhibition by Ilya and Emilia Kabakov. Half way through the exhibits there was a closed door, a woman on a chair guarding it – much like the women who used to sit outside toilets in Prague taking a few crowns, handing out a piece of toilet paper. The woman nodded me in and I was faced by a corridor.

74. Výměnek

Part of a smallholding given to grandparents, aka granny flat.

Reviews of THE GOOSE WOMAN

Kirwan observes the world with a ferocious tenderness and profound attentiveness. Her poems capture the rhythms and exquisite details of domesticity and erotic love, the mysterious surfaces of physical experience, the powerful undercurrents of memory, dream and desire that shape and connect us.

Her latest collection suspends a washing line from the west coast of Ireland of her childhood to the village in Central Bohemia where she now spends much of her time, living in the former home of the eponymous goose woman. The poems suspended from this line are astonishingly immediate, with a Keatsian relish for the sensuous, reflecting her passionate relationship with the "strong and steady man" who built their home, her unsentimental empathy for the goose woman, who "hated anyone further than Rousinov, / especially Praguers who drove by her front step / when she was plucking a goose", her drily humorous observation of the whisperings, preoccupations and prejudices of village life in both Ireland and the Czech Republic and her complex connection with the histories of both countries.

In a poem inspired by a Richard Long sculpture in Connemara, 'Those Left Behind', Kirwan writes that " – all we can do is witness, / our outlines are vivid, even the trees." and the acutely observed poems collected in *The Goose Woman* are poems of urgent, vivid, moving and profoundly human witness.

Bernie Higgins

Both the poet and the wild bees are 'exiled' and confused in *Slabce*, an unimportant village in Central Bohemia. The bees are confused because of the concrete the poet's partner pours everywhere as he rebuilds a ruined farmhouse, she because she's displaced, has always lived in a city. Yet she is calmed by the countryside, becomes a fascinated observer, watching closely, appreciating what might be common, unpleasant or unnoticeable for Czech eyes, searching for beauty and importance in invisible things and people.

Their aged and surly neighbour, a goose woman, becomes an icon of the dilapidating village, representing a knot from which threads of memories can be traced. She provides the narrator with evidence of life passing – from flashes of the poet's mother and grandmother, to varied kinds of necessities and longings, even erotic ones like the beautiful fantasy in "The [young and naked] Goose Woman Considers".

Despite some existential resistance and disbelief, there begins a new life for the narrator. Restoring the house is intertwined with love, the house becomes an anchor, the garden is respectfully controlled nature, yet remains uncontrollable. *The Goose Woman,* with its wonderfully clever composition, is a book of poems that are not just sensuous metaphors but stories. The nest of a 'Bohemian Redstart' blocks the door to the kitchen: "occasionally/ we catch him   in flight/ flash of red   dandy flash   that   *watch me"*.

Eva Kalivodová

ABOUT THE AUTHOR

Jane Kirwan was born in Northampton of Irish parents, qualified as a dentist then did an English degree. She divides her time between London and the Czech Republic. Her poetry collections *Stealing the Eiffel Tower* (1997), *The Man Who Sold Mirrors* (2003) and *Second Exile* (2010) (poems and prose written with Ales Macháček), were published by Rockingham Press. She won an Arts Council Writers' Award in 2002, has been commended and won prizes in several competitions including the National and Hippocrates, has read on Czech TV and at festivals in the UK and abroad. *Born in the NHS,* a collection of poetry and prose (Hippocrates Press 2013), was written with Wendy French. A novel *Don't Mention Her* (2016) and poetry *Stories & Lies* (with Pam Johnson, Jennifer Grigg, 2018) were published by Blue Door Press.

FORTHCOMING FROM BLUE DOOR PRESS

Snow on the Danube by Francis Gilbert

Hidden by Annabel Chown

BLUE DOOR PRESS publications

Herrings: a poetry anthology

Stories & Lies: poetry by P Johnson, J Kirwan, J Grigg

Taking in Water: a novel by Pamela Johnson

Don't Mention Her : a novel by Jane Kirwan

Who Do You Love: a novel by Francis Gilbert

ABOUT BLUE DOOR PRESS

Blue Door Press is a co-publishing venture involving writers, editors and designers with the aim of producing high-quality, thought-provoking books – fiction, memoir and poetry. The Press published its first literary fiction in 2016. More fiction and memoir is planned for 2019.

www.bluedoorpress.co.uk

MORE ABOUT FORTHCOMING TITLES

Hidden: a memoir by Annabel Chown

Aged 31, Annabel was diagnosed with breast cancer. At the time a successful architect with a busy London social life, this came as tremendous shock. In *Hidden,* Chown charts each stage of the treatment and her growing understanding of different kinds of architecture – those of her own body and the structure of the life she'd built up. Is this what she wants?

Snow on the Danube: a novel by Francis Gilbert

Snow on the Danube evokes the lost world of Budapest during and between two great wars and is recounted in the inimitable voice of Count Zoltán Pongrácz: a fussy hypochondriac who becomes an unlikely and compromised hero when the fascists take over his beloved country. An unlikely comedy, a document of filial love and a compelling portrait of the horrors of war, *Snow on the Danube* is the story of one man's quest to save everything he loves most: his family, his friends – and, perhaps, his soul.

www.ingramcontent.com/pod-product-compliance
Lightning Source LLC
Chambersburg PA
CBHW031452040426
42444CB00007B/1073